As You Like It

A Shakespeare Story

RETOLD BY ANDREW MATTHEWS
ILLUSTRATED BY TONY ROSS

ORCHARD

For Sheena, with all my love
A.M.

ORCHARD BOOKS
338 Euston Road, London NW1 3BH
Orchard Books Australia
Hachette Children's Books
Level 17/207 Kent St, Sydney, NSW 2000
First published in Great Britain in 2006
First paperback publication in 2007
This slipcase edition published in 2013
Not for individual resale
Text © Andrew Matthews 2006
Illustrations © Tony Ross 2006
ISBN 978 1 40780 980 9
The rights of Andrew Matthews to be identified as the author and Tony Ross as
the illustrator of this work have been asserted by them in accordance with the
Copyright, Designs and Patents Act, 1988.
A CIP catalogue record for this book is available from the British Library
Printed in China

Orchard Books is a division of Hachette Childrens Books,
an Hachette UK company.
www.hachette.co.uk

Contents

Cast List

Duke Senior

Living in banishment

Rosalind

Duke Senior's daughter

Duke Frederick

Duke Senior's brother

Celia

Duke Frederick's daughter

Orlando

Youngest son of Sir Rowland de Boys

The Scene

France in the sixteenth century.

Under the greenwood tree,
Who loves to lie with me,
And turn his merry note
Unto the sweet bird's throat:
Come hither, come hither, come hither.
Here shall he see
No enemy
But winter and rough weather.

Amiens; II.v.

As You Like It

When Duke Senior was banished by his
brother, Frederick, many loyal courtiers
followed him into the Forest of Arden.
Here they lived simply, hunting game and
gathering wild fruits. The forest gave them
a leafy roof, and mossy beds to sleep on.

Duke Senior found himself more content than he had ever been before.

Duke Frederick's life was not so pleasant. He was plagued by guilt, and grew suspicious of all those around him, especially his niece, Rosalind. Rosalind had not gone into exile with her father because Celia, Duke Frederick's only child, had begged for her to stay as a playmate. Celia and Rosalind became firm friends.

But as the girls grew into young women, Duke Frederick began to notice how Rosalind outshone his daughter. Rosalind's chestnut-brown hair and green eyes attracted more admiring glances than Celia's blonde ringlets and dimpled smile.

Duke Frederick's resentment of his niece festered inside him. He was determined that if Rosalind gave him the slightest excuse, he would banish her.

✳ ✳ ✳

One fine morning, Celia and Rosalind
visited a village fair on their way home
from riding. There they met Le Beau, one
of the duke's courtiers.

"Ladies, you're just in time!" he
declared. "The duke has offered a purse
of fifty ducats to any man who can throw
his wrestler Charles. Two challengers have
been carried away groaning. The last
contender is a charming young fellow.

Everybody wants him to win, but it's more likely that Charles will break his neck."

Celia and Rosalind were intrigued enough to follow Le Beau to the wrestling ground.

A crowd had gathered around a circle marked out on the grass. Within the circle stood Charles, whose powerful shoulders and flattened nose made him seem more like an ox than a man.

Duke Frederick emerged
from the crowd and walked
over to his daughter and
niece. He kissed Celia's
cheek; Rosalind received
the slightest of nods.

"I'm glad you're here,"
said the duke. "A brave
but foolish young stranger
insists on fighting my
wrestling
champion.

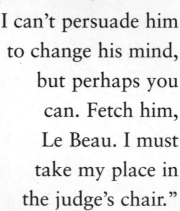

I can't persuade him
to change his mind,
but perhaps you
can. Fetch him,
Le Beau. I must
take my place in
the judge's chair."

The young man Le Beau presented to
Celia and Rosalind was dressed in a dark
green doublet and hose. He was tall and
athletic, with a mass of blond hair, and
clear grey-blue eyes.

Rosalind felt giddy.

"Do you really mean to fight the duke's
wrestler, sir?" she asked.

"I do, my lady," said the stranger.

"I wish you wouldn't!" blurted Rosalind. "You could be badly injured."

"I wish you wouldn't too!" Celia said. "Charles might ruin your handsome— I mean, you could be killed."

The stranger smiled sadly. "I'm touched by your concern, ladies. But the truth is

that I need that purse of ducats," he said.
"If I'm injured or killed, so be it. I have
no family or friends to care whether I live
or die."

"I care!" thought Rosalind, and her
heart went out to the lonely young man.

A trumpeter blew a fanfare, and the
stranger returned to the wrestling ring.

"Begin!" Duke Frederick commanded.
The wrestlers circled warily. Charles
made several lunges, but the stranger
evaded his grip, turning and sidestepping
as gracefully as a dancer. Charles seemed
lumbering in comparison, and the crowd
laughed at him. The laughter angered
Charles, and anger made him careless.

In a move almost too swift to follow, the stranger seized Charles around the waist and threw him to the ground, where he lay dazed and winded.

The crowd cheered wildly, until Duke Frederick stood up from his chair and signalled for silence.

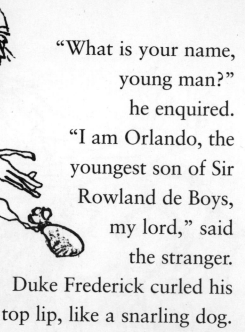

"What is your name,
young man?"
he enquired.
"I am Orlando, the
youngest son of Sir
Rowland de Boys,
my lord," said
the stranger.
Duke Frederick curled his
top lip, like a snarling dog.
"Your late father was my sworn
enemy!" he rasped, flinging
a purse at Orlando's
feet. "Take your money
and go!" He turned to
a courtier. "Have
Charles carried to a
physician. Celia,
come with me!"

The duke stormed off with Le Beau in attendance. Celia, her face crimson with embarrassment at the duke's behaviour, scampered after her father.

The crowd melted away, and soon only Orlando and Rosalind were left. Rosalind stepped forward, unfastened a gold chain from around her neck and held it out.

"Will you wear this, and think of me sometimes, sir?" she said.

As Orlando took the chain, his mind went blank.

"My lady, I – I – I," he gabbled.

"I knew your father," said Rosalind. "He was a gallant gentleman."

She reached up and brushed her fingertips against Orlando's cheek, then hurried off. "What?" Orlando thought. "Who? Why?"

"A word with you, sir," someone
murmured.

Orlando turned, and saw that Le Beau
had returned to the wrestling ground.

"Why is Sir Rowland's son wrestling
at a village fair?" Le Beau asked.

Orlando sighed.

"My older brother
Oliver refuses to share
our inheritance," he
said. "He drove me
out at the point of
a sword, and swore
that he would have me
murdered if I ever came back."

"You're no safer here," confided Le Beau.
"The duke is in one of his
black rages, and means
to do you mischief.
Go to the Forest of
Arden, and find
Duke Senior. That's
what I would do, if
I had the nerve."
"Thanks for your
advice, friend,"

Orlando said. "But before I leave, who
was the dark-haired lady who spoke to
me just now?"

"The old duke's daughter, Rosalind,"
Le Beau informed him.

"Rosalind," thought Orlando. "A pretty
name. A lovely name. A *wonderful* name!"

And all at once, the danger he was in
did not seem to matter in the least.

At the same time as Orlando was setting out for the Forest of Arden, in the garden of the duke's mansion, Celia was staring in disbelief at her cousin.

"How can you be in love with Orlando?" she exclaimed. "You've only just met him!"

"Yet I know we're meant for each other," said Rosalind.

Just then Duke Frederick appeared, his brows bent into a fearsome frown. "Leave my house, Rosalind!" he barked. "You have five days to quit the dukedom. If you're found within twenty miles of here after that, you'll be put to death."

Rosalind's face paled.

"What have I done to deserve this, uncle?" she asked.

"You were talking to the son of my old enemy!" the duke ranted. "No doubt you were plotting to get rid of me and replace me with your father."

"I did no such thing, my lord," Rosalind said calmly.

"Rosalind would no more plot against you than I would, father!" protested Celia.

Flecks of foam formed at the corners of the duke's mouth. "Can you be such a fool, Celia?" he hissed. "Don't you see how she simpers her way into people's affections, so that they praise her and mock you? Rosalind must leave or die."

Duke Frederick wheeled round, and marched back to the mansion.

"He's gone mad!" whispered Celia.
"What will you do, cousin?"

"I have no choice but to leave,"
Rosalind said. "I'll go to Arden and
search for my father."

"And I'll come with you," said Celia.
"I'm not staying here with a madman.
I've enough money to last us
a long while, and—"
She paused, and
gnawed at her
bottom lip.
"But how
will we
manage the
journey?
Two young
women won't
be safe alone."

Rosalind clapped her hands as
inspiration came to her.

"Wear a country girl's clothes!" she
said. "I'll cut my hair, dress as a man and
call myself Ganymede."

"And I'll be Aliena!" said Celia.

The cousins laughed like children
at play.

Some weeks later, Duke Senior and his followers were seated around a campfire, eating their evening meal. Jaques, a gloomy nobleman, was spouting an opinion that no one had asked for.

"Life is a stage on which we play many parts," he said. "First we're babies, warm and wet at both ends, then we're schoolchildren, dragging ourselves to lessons. Next we play young lovers, who mope about, writing ridiculous poetry.

Then we're soldiers, diving into the mouths of cannon to prove our courage. In middle age, we grow fat and bore the young with our wisdom. Lastly we shrink into the role of the elderly, toothless and deaf, and then we make our final exit, never to return."

"Thank you, Jaques," said a nobleman on the opposite side of the fire. "Listening to you always cheers me up."

"Hello – who's there?" called out another.

Orlando advanced into the firelight, hands raised to show that he held no weapon.

"Forgive me, gentlemen," he said. "I'd given myself up for lost until I saw your fire."

"What are you doing wandering in the forest at night?" demanded Jaques.

"Searching for Duke Senior," said Orlando.

"And you have found him," Duke Senior said. "What is your name, young sir?"

Orlando bowed. "I am Orlando, youngest son of—"

"Sir Rowland de Boys!" laughed Duke Senior. "I see your father's face in yours, my boy. You're welcome for his sake, as well as your own. Sit down, eat, and tell us the story of how you come to be here."

"And tell it quickly, before Jaques starts up again!" a voice pleaded.

* * *

For over a month, Celia and Rosalind had
been living in a cottage near the edge of the
forest. They rented the cottage from a local
farmer, who kept them supplied with
produce. Good food and fresh air had
altered the cousins' appearance. Both had
tanned faces, and the sun had brought out
lighter streaks in Rosalind's bobbed hair.

Rosalind had been unable to locate her father, but unhappy thoughts of Orlando weighed most heavily on her mind. One afternoon, while they were strolling aimlessly along a forest track, Rosalind poured her heart out to Celia.

"What if Orlando falls in love with someone else?" she fretted.

"He won't," Celia assured her. "Not if he loves you as truly as you love him."

"But I don't know if he loves me!" wailed Rosalind.

"I think I saw love in his eyes, but he didn't say anything. And how will we meet again? He could be anywhere!"

"Don't give up hope," said Celia. "Love is sure to find a way." She stopped walking and cocked her head to one side. "Can you hear that scratching, mumbling sound? It's coming from over there." Cautiously, the young women peered through the branches of a thick clump of bushes.

Rosalind almost shouted with joy, for
there was Orlando, lying on his stomach
in the centre of a glade. He dipped a quill
pen into a deer-horn inkwell, and
muttered to himself as he scribbled on
a piece of parchment.

"Fly to him, Rosalind!" urged Celia. "Swear your undying love."

Rosalind arched an eyebrow and smiled mischievously.

"I'm not caught as easily as that," she said. "Let's find out how good an actor I am. Let me do the talking."

Orlando began to recite what he had written.

> *"When through the treetops*
> *blows the wind,*
> *It speaks the name of Rosalind.*

Fish in the river, webby-finned,
Sing of the beauty of fair Rosalind."

"Is that supposed to be a love poem?"
said Rosalind, stepping into the glade
with Celia at her side.

Orlando started, and shot a sour
look at what he assumed was a badly
mannered youth.

"Yes, not that it has anything to do with you," he said. "Who are you?"

"I'm Ganymede, this is my sister, Aliena," Rosalind told him. "We live in a cottage down the way. How can fish sing when they live underwater?"

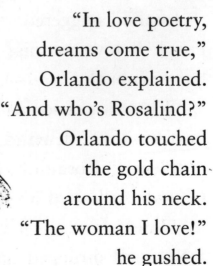

"In love poetry, dreams come true," Orlando explained. "And who's Rosalind?" Orlando touched the gold chain around his neck. "The woman I love!" he gushed.

Rosalind sniggered. "You're not in love! People in love are miserable, but you look happy enough."

"What would you know of love, insolent boy?" demanded Orlando.

"Plenty!" Rosalind said. "It's a disease. I cured a fellow of it once."

"How?"

Rosalind shrugged casually.

"I pretended to be his ladylove," she
said. "First I flirted, then I argued. I was
cruel, kind, spiteful and gentle. I kept
leading him on and putting him off. In the
end, he was so sick of love that he made a
full recovery. I could do the same for you."

Orlando shook his head. "I don't want
to be cured."

"Of course you do," said Rosalind.

"That poem of yours was a cry for help
if ever I heard one. Come to my cottage
every day, and I'll cure you in a week."

Orlando found the idea amusing.

"Where is your cottage?" he said.

"I'll show you. Follow me," said Rosalind.

"Very well, lad."

"Now, now!" scolded Rosalind, wagging
a finger. "You call me *Rosalind* from now
on, agreed?"

"Agreed, fair Rosalind," said Orlando.

Next morning, Orlando found Rosalind pacing up and down outside the cottage.

"Good day, Ganymede – er, fair Rosalind!" Orlando said.

Rosalind looked down her nose at him.

"You're an hour late!" she snapped. "Is this how you show a lady your love, by keeping her waiting?" Orlando bowed low.

"Forgive me, my Rosalind."

"When did I say that I was yours?" Rosalind asked sharply.

"I wish you were!" sighed Orlando.

"Then sweet-talk me."

Orlando leaned closer.

"I'd rather kiss before we talk," he purred.

Rosalind stepped back.

"Certainly not!" she exclaimed. "Talk first, and you might get a kiss after we run out of things to say."

Orlando sank down on one knee.

"Marry me, Rosalind!"
he begged.

Rosalind looked directly
into Orlando's eyes.

"When I marry you, I'll
love you with all my heart,
and I'll be true to you
alone," she vowed. "If your Rosalind
were here, she would say the same."

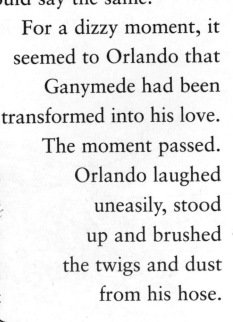

For a dizzy moment, it
seemed to Orlando that
Ganymede had been
transformed into his love.
The moment passed.
Orlando laughed
uneasily, stood
up and brushed
the twigs and dust
from his hose.

"I must leave you for a while," he said. "I promised Duke Senior that I would dine with him."

"Duke Senior?" gasped Rosalind. "Is his camp nearby?"

"It's easy to find, if you know where to look," Orlando said airily. "Farewell, sweet Rosalind. I promise to return at two o'clock."

"Don't be late!" said Rosalind.

After Orlando had gone, Celia came out of the cottage.

"Oh, Celia, I can't pretend much longer! I love Orlando so much," declared Rosalind, and burst into tears.

"Why are you crying?" Celia enquired.

"Because I'm so happy!"

"I don't think I'll ever understand this love business," Celia said to herself.

But she was to learn all about love before too long.

✳ ✳ ✳

Two o'clock came and went with no
sign of Orlando. Rosalind sat on the
doorstep of the cottage and sulked, while
Celia hung out washing.

Celia noticed a handsome gentleman
coming down the track. The gentleman
walked up to her and doffed his cap.

"Are you Aliena?" he asked, blushing.

"I am, sir," replied Celia, also blushing.

"And is that the youth who calls himself *Rosalind*?" the gentleman continued.

"It is," said Rosalind. The gentleman held up a bloodstained cloth.

"Orlando told me to show you this, and to explain why he hasn't kept his appointment," he said. Rosalind frowned. "How do you know Orlando's business?"

"I am his brother Oliver," the gentleman confessed.

"This morning I was travelling on foot
through the forest. I stopped to rest and
fell into a deep sleep. Orlando happened
to pass just as a lioness was about to
pounce on me. Without knowing who
I was, and with no thought for himself,
he charged the beast to drive it off.

The lioness's savage roaring woke me.
When I saw how nobly and courageously
Orlando had acted, I realised how
shamefully I've treated him. Our quarrel is
over. I have sworn to Duke Senior that
I will give my brother half of all I own."

Rosalind pointed at the cloth.

"Where did that blood come from?" she said. "It is Orlando's," Oliver told her. "Before she ran away, the lioness clawed his arm. Luckily he's in no danger. The duke's physician is bandaging his wound." Rosalind sprang to her feet.

"I must go to him!" she exclaimed.
"No, wait. Sir, tell your brother to bring
Duke Senior and his men to the chapel
just outside the forest tomorrow at noon.
I'll bring his true Rosalind there, and they
will be married."

Rosalind broke into a run.

"Where are you going?" called Celia.

"To find a priest – and a dress!"
Rosalind cried.

In the silence that followed Rosalind's departure, Oliver and Celia shyly eyed each other.

"So, there's to be a wedding tomorrow," Oliver said.

"Yes, sir," said Celia.

"Tell me, beautiful Aliena," Oliver said, "have you ever thought of getting married?"

Celia's eyes sparkled.

"Not until now, sir!' she said.

* * *

The following day, at the chapel, there was rejoicing when Duke Senior was reunited with his beloved daughter. Surprises followed. Orlando roared with laughter when Rosalind revealed the truth about Ganymede, and Oliver was bemused to learn that his bride-to-be was actually named Celia.

The happy couples were on the point of
entering the chapel, when Le Beau
galloped up on a dapple-grey mare. The
courtier slipped from his saddle and
bowed to Duke Senior.

"My lord, Duke Frederick came to the forest last night with a troop of soldiers," he said. "He meant to track you down and kill you. Instead, he met a holy hermit who spoke many words of wisdom to him. As a result, Duke Frederick returns your title and estates. He has joined a monastery."

"And so shall I!" Jaques announced. "It's far too happy here for my liking."

But it was only the start of that day's happiness. The celebrations went on late into the night, and every bough in the forest rang with singing and laughter.

If I were a woman, I would kiss as many of you as had beards that pleased me...

Rosalind; V.iv.

Nature and Identity in As You Like It

Shakespeare wrote *As You Like It* between 1599 and 1600. He took the plot from *Rosalynde* by Thomas Lodge, which was based on the medieval *Tale of Gamelyn*, thought to be the work of Geoffrey Chaucer.

The play opens darkly. Orlando's life is threatened, and he is forced to flee his home. In the course of his wanderings, Orlando meets and falls in love with Rosalind, the niece of the demented Duke Frederick. The duke exiles Rosalind, an act which costs him the respect and love of his daughter, Celia. Rosalind and Celia disguise themselves and travel to the Forest of Arden to search for Rosalind's father, the banished Duke Senior.

Once the scene shifts to the forest, the play

is transformed. The power of Nature heals all wounds. Lovers are reunited – and discovered. Duke Frederick undergoes a religious conversion and reinstates Duke Senior before joining a monastery. The Forest of Arden is a place of miracles, not least of which is that lions live there!

On the Elizabethan stage, all female parts were acted by young boys. So, in the scenes between Ganymede and Orlando, the actor playing Ganymede/Rosalind would have been a boy pretending to be a girl, who is pretending to be a boy pretending to be a girl.

All this makes no difference to the audience's enjoyment. The play is not intended to be realistic. It is set in a world where disguises convince everybody, villains have sudden changes of heart, and love always wins in the end. Shakespeare presents life not as it is, but how it ought to be – as we would like it, in fact.

Shakespeare and the Globe Theatre

Some of Shakespeare's most famous plays were first performed at the Globe Theatre, which was built on the South Bank of the River Thames in 1599.

Going to the Globe was a different experience from going to the theatre today. The building was roughly circular in shape, but with flat sides: a little like a doughnut crossed with a fifty-pence piece. Because the Globe was an open-air theatre, plays were only put on during daylight hours in spring and summer. People paid a penny to stand in the central space and watch a play, and this part of the audience became known as 'the groundlings' because they stood on the ground. A place in the tiers of seating beneath the thatched roof, where there was a slightly better view and less chance of being rained on, cost extra.

The Elizabethans did not bath very often and the audiences at the Globe were smelly. Fine ladies and gentlemen in the more expensive seats sniffed perfume and bags of sweetly scented herbs to cover the stink rising from the groundlings.

There were no actresses on the stage; all the female characters in Shakespeare's plays would have been acted by boys, wearing wigs and make-up. Audiences were not well behaved. People clapped and cheered when their favourite actors came on stage; bad actors were jeered at and sometimes pelted with whatever came to hand.

Most Londoners worked hard to make a living and in their precious free time they liked to be entertained. Shakespeare understood the magic of the theatre so well that today, almost four hundred years after his death, his plays still cast a spell over the thousands of people that go to see them.

Orchard Classics
Shakespeare Stories

RETOLD BY ANDREW MATTHEWS
ILLUSTRATED BY TONY ROSS

As You Like It	978 1 84616 187 2	£4.99
Hamlet	978 1 84121 340 8	£4.99
A Midsummer Night's Dream	978 1 84121 332 3	£4.99
Antony and Cleopatra	978 1 84121 338 5	£4.99
The Tempest	978 1 84121 346 0	£4.99
Richard III	978 1 84616 185 8	£4.99
Macbeth	978 1 84121 344 6	£4.99
Twelfth Night	978 1 84121 334 7	£4.99
Henry V	978 1 84121 342 2	£4.99
Romeo & Juliet	978 1 84121 336 1	£4.99
Much Ado About Nothing	978 1 84616 183 4	£4.99
Othello	978 1 84616 184 1	£4.99
Julius Caesar	978 1 40830 506 5	£4.99
King Lear	978 1 40830 503 4	£4.99
The Merchant of Venice	978 1 40830 504 1	£4.99
The Taming of the Shrew	978 1 40830 505 8	£4.99

Orchard Books are available from all good bookshops.